GOD WILL NEVER STOP LOVING YOU

BECAUSE OF WHAT JESUS DID FOR YOU!

ROSEMARY F. OKOLO

Unless otherwise indicated, all scripture quotations are taken from the Holy Bible, Amplified Version. (AMP)

GOD WILL NEVER STOP LOVING YOU

Because of what Jesus did for you

Copyright © 2015 Rosemary Okolo

ISBN- 13: 978 1519470744
ISBN- 10: 1519470746

Second publishing

Rosemary Okolo Ministries

www.rosemaryokolo.org

Published in Partnership with:

Infallible Word Ministries

Nottingham, United Kingdom

www.infallibleword.org.uk

We are committed to reaching people and changing lives partly, through publishing great, thought provoking books based on the Bible that would connect you to the truth of God's Word. It is our prayer that this book would be a blessing to you!

For more information or to purchase other products from Rosemary Okolo and Infallible Word Ministries, please contact us at the addresses above.

All rights reserved under International copyright Law. No part of this book may be reproduced, stored in a retrieval system, or transmitted by any means without the prior written permission of the author.

Other books by Rosemary F. Okolo

Take Charge of your Circumstances: by the Power of Your Words

Raising the Giant in you: A Guide Book for Every Youth

Grant no access: Understanding the subtle trap of the enemy

An Errand of Grace. A Novel

Adira. (A reviewed copy of An Errand of Grace for Young adult readers).

Speak the Word in the face of your circumstances

www.rosemaryokolo.org

ACKNOWLEDGEMENTS

Special thanks to my Husband Charles Okolo. Thank you for encouraging me to write this little book to be used as a Ministry tool for Infallible Word Ministries. A Ministry founded through the Grace of God, to teach and preach the uncompromising truth of God's Word and His unconditional love to all with integrity.

Thank you for your love, prayers, support and encouragement and for your awesome dedication to our family. I couldn't have accomplished this and anything else without your support.

I am so honoured to have you in my life. I love you forever. And as always, I thank God for entrusting me with His Grace!

GOD WILL NEVER STOP LOVING YOU

Because of what Jesus did for you!

TABLE OF CONTENTS

Introduction 1

Chapter 1 God loves you 5

Chapter 2 you matter to God 11

Chapter 3 God will never stop loving you 17

Chapter 4 God can still reach you 28

Chapter 5 God does not send anyone to hell 42

Chapter 6 God wants relationship with you 53

About the author 64

Introduction

Sadly, religion has thought us for so long that, we have to earn God's love. That, we have to do right, and live right before God could ever love us. That, we have to work as hard as we can through our performances in order to please God and get Him to love us or before we can receive His love.

Religion has thought us that, if we are not good enough and get our lives together, we cannot earn God's love! No wonder, some people have made statements such as, "God only helps those who help themselves." These are all lies from the pit of hell and are not recorded in the Bible.

First of all, we cannot help ourselves without God's grace. We cannot live right or get our lives together without Him and neither can we please God in ourselves in the flesh. In other words, no one can make God to love them and no one can please God without faith in Him through His Son Jesus Christ.

We were so unworthy and so helpless when God came to show us His great love for us through His Son Jesus. He hates sin and cannot be pleased or delighted in anyway by our sins but God loves you and me in spite of us.

In other words, His love for us is not dependent on what we do or what we don't do. It's not dependent on our performances, our living right or not living right, our lifestyles, our achievements and successes. It's not dependent on anything but on Who He is!

He just loves us because, He is Love. His very nature is love and He has promised to love us regardless! He still loved us so very much even in that terrible state we were in, without Christ. He knew we couldn't help ourselves. No one can help themselves without God's grace.

The Word of God clearly declares in John 3:16 that, for God so loved the world – (you, me and everyone) that He gave His only begotten Son that, whosoever believes in Him should not perish but have everlasting life. For, while we were yet sinners, Christ died for us!

Friend, we did not deserve and cannot earn God's love for us. No one can. God chose to love us even before the foundations of the earth. He chose to love us even before we ever thought about Him or knew Him.

He chose to love you and me even in our state of sin, unrighteousness and wickedness.

It was His great love for us that moved Him through compassion for us, to send His beloved Son Jesus Christ, into the world to die a brutal death for us on the cross, in other to redeem us from the curse of the law, from the wages of sin which is eternal death and hell. And to redeem us back to God so we can have a great relationship with Him and enjoy life to the full.

Friend, God loves you and He will never stop loving you because of what Jesus did for you! My prayer is that, as you turn the pages of this little book, you will get an understanding of God's great love for you. That, you will come to realise that His thoughts towards you, are to do you good.

That, He wants the best for you and He has done everything for you to receive His love, and His best, through His Son Jesus. It is my hope that you will not only be blessed as you read this little book, but that you will receive God's unconditional love into your heart! God loves YOU!

In His Service,

Rosemary Okolo

Chapter one

GOD LOVES YOU!

Friend, God loves you! He loves you beyond your wildest thoughts and imaginations. He loves you far beyond your human mind could ever comprehend. He loves you with an everlasting love.

You see, His love has no boundaries, transcends and, cuts across race, colour, culture, age, sex and so much more. He loves you with an unconditional love. Now, how do I know these? Because the Bible, God's Word tells me so.

"For God so loved the world that, He sent His only begotten Son, that whosoever believes in Him should not perish but have everlasting life." (John 3:16 NKJV)

"For God so greatly loved and dearly prized the world that He [even] gave up His only begotten (unique) Son, so that whosoever believes in (trusts

in, clings to, relies on) Him shall not perish (come to destruction, be lost) but have eternal (everlasting) life." (John 3:16)

"But God shows and clearly proves His *[own]* love for us by the fact that, while we were still sinners, Christ (the Messiah, the Anointed One) died for us." *(Romans 5:8).*

Friend, God demonstrated His great, awesome love for you and me by sending His Son Jesus Christ to die for you and me on the cross for our sins. This is the boldest, greatest expression of His love for us.

God loved you and still loves you even before you were born into this world, before you ever heard about Him and even when you were at odds with Him. He already loved you and still loves you so very much with an unconditional love.

Suffice to say that, the greatest expression and picture of God's love for you and me is Jesus' crucifixion for us. The Bible says in the book of Romans 5:6-8 that, at just the right time, when we were still powerless, weak and unable to help ourselves, Jesus died for us, who were ungodly, wicked, selfish and self - centred.

But God demonstrates, His own love for us by sending His only begotten Son Jesus, to die for us. This was a clear, unmistakable declaration of His love for us.

"While we were yet in weakness [powerless to help ourselves], at the fitting time, Christ died for (in behalf of) the ungodly. Now it is an extraordinary thing for one to give his life even for an upright man, though perhaps for a noble and lovable and generous benefactor someone might even dare to die.

But God shows and clearly proves his [own] love for us by the fact that while we were still sinners, Christ 9the messiah, the Anointed One) died for us." (Romans 5:6-8)

Jesus did it for you and for me! He did it for us. How awesome and wonderful is that! He chose to do it for us, to die for us regardless of the state we were in. He did it for you and me. Hallelujah!

"No one has greater love [no one has shown stronger affection] than to lay down (give up) his own life for his friends. (John 15:13).

This is unconditional love! Friend, God loves you so very much and cares about you. He is a good God and wants to do you only good. He wants to show you His love, mercy and goodness. He wants to show you His faithfulness.

"For the Lord is good; His faithfulness and truth endure to all generations." (Psalms 100:5)

"For God is sheer beauty, all – generous in love, loyal always and forever." (MSG)

"And you He made alive, who were dead in trespasses and sins..., but God, who is rich in mercy, because of His great love with which He loved us, even when we were dead in trespasses, made us alive together with Christ..." (Ephesians 2:1, 4-5 NKJV)

Friend, I don't know exactly where you are at right now, as you turn and read the pages of this little book, but one thing I do know and of which I am very certain of is this, that God truly loves you!

God really loves you more than anyone could ever love you and far beyond what you could ever think or imagine. He loves you and He says in His Word clearly, that He loves you.

He is not a man that He would lie to you, nor a mere man that He would change His mind or His moods about you. He is not schizophrenic neither does He have a mood swing like natural men do. He is true to His Word and His Word is His bond. He says what He means and He means what He says.

You can trust Him and depend on Him. His love for you will never change, fade or fail. Only believe this and receive His unconditional love for you right now, where you are. Regardless of where you are right now, always know this that, God loves you so very much!

"God is not a man that He should tell or act a lie, neither the son of man, that He should feel repentance or compunction [for what He has promised]. Has he said and shall He not do it? Or

has He spoken and shall He not make it good?" (Numbers 23:19)

Chapter two

YOU MATTER TO GOD

Friend, you matter to God! You are so valuable to Him. You are His masterpiece. You are not worthless and a useless nobody. You are awesome, beautiful, precious and special.

You are talented, gifted and you are one of a kind. You really do matter to God and so valuable in His sight. You are wonderfully and fearfully made.

"O Lord, You have examined my heart and know everything about me. You know when I sit down or stand up. You know my thoughts even when I'm far away. You see me when I travel and when I rest at home.

You know everything I do. You know what I am going to say even before I say it, Lord. You go before me and follow me. You place your hand of blessing on my head. Such knowledge is too wonderful for me, too great for me to understand!"

"Thank you for making me so wonderfully complex! Your workmanship is marvellous – how well I know it... How precious are your thoughts about me, o God. They cannot be numbered!" (Psalms 139:1-6; 14, 17 NLT)

You see, regardless of your past mistakes, regardless of all your negative experiences, God still loves you and cares about you. He wants the best for you. And no matter how poorly you think of yourself, God thinks highly of you. His thoughts towards you and about you are great thoughts.

Thoughts to make you smile and be happy. Thoughts that would raise your self-esteem, cause you to square your shoulders and walk with confidence, thoughts that would make you feel good about yourself. God still loves you regardless of what you have done and He has a great plan and future for your life!

"For I know the plans I have for you," says the Lord. "They are plans for good and not for disaster,

to give you a future and a hope." (Jeremiah 29:11 NLT)

"...since you were precious in my sight, you have been honoured, and I have loved you...! (Isaiah 43:4 NKJV)

You may think and feel that nobody knows you, and maybe so, but the Bible says that, God knows you. He knows where you live, He knows your name, He knows everything about you and yet, He says that He still loves you so much and that you matter to Him, regardless.

How awesome is that! You see, God kept you, you are alive because He loves you and has a great plan for your life, a plan that only you can fulfil. God created you with greatness inside of you and He created you for a reason.

And regardless of all that the devil has put you through, regardless of all the ups and downs and negative experiences you have had to go through, which didn't come from God but from the devil, God still loves you and cares about you.

You do matter to Him! Bad things don't come from God but from the devil and through our wrong choices. God is good and remains good forever.

"The thief comes only in order to steal and kill and destroy. I came that they may have and enjoy life, and have it in abundance (to the full, till it overflows.)"

"...yes, I have loved you with an everlasting love; therefore, with loving kindness I have drawn you. Again, I will build you, and you shall be rebuilt..," (Jeremiah 31:3-4 NKJV)

God wants to step into your life and love you like you have never ever been loved before. You were not and you are not an accident. You were created by God. He made you the way you are, He designed you with all the intricate details of your life, to love you.

He wants to be an important part of your everyday life. You matter to God! You matter to God because, God sent His Son, Jesus Christ to die on the cross for you. Yes, it was for someone like you that Jesus came to die for.

You do matter to God. And He wants you to feel good, secure and confident about yourself, in who you are and in who He created you to be.

"Before I formed you in the womb I knew [and] approved of you [as my chosen instrument], and before you were born I separated and set you apart, consecrating you; [and] I appointed you a prophet to the nations." (Jeremiah 1:5)

Right now, you may feel you don't measure up and you feel condemned but friend, don't be your own worst enemy. God knows your every weakness and still loves you anyway.

He wants the very best for you because, He loves you so very much. And above all, He wants to have a relationship with Him. He wants you to know Him for yourself as He really is, and you are so worth it, and worth so much in His sight.

However, you have to believe all He says about you in His Word, (the Bible) and receive His amazing love for you and then, love yourself. You can't even love someone else if you do not love yourself.

Friend, God created you and me so He could have relationship and fellowship with us and love us! I hope you will get to know Him very soon. You matter to God. You are valuable, precious and worthy of His love and you matter to God.

Why? Because of what Jesus did for you when He gave His precious life for you and me, for us at the cross of Calvary. You are precious to God and you do matter to God!

"Look at the birds of the air, they neither sow nor reap nor gather into barns, and yet your Heavenly Father keeps feeding them. Are you not worth much more than they?" (Matthew 6:26)

Regardless of what you are going through or where you are at right now, never ever forget this that, you matter so very much to God, you are so valuable and precious in His sight and He will never ever stop loving you because of what Jesus Christ did for you!

Chapter three

GOD WILL NEVER STOP LOVING YOU

God doesn't have love, He is love. His very nature is love, that's Who He is and no matter how much you run away from Him, no matter how you hurt Him and continue in sin, He will never stop loving you because of what Jesus did for you. He will continue to love you regardless.

There is nothing you can do to stop God from loving you because of what Jesus Christ did for you over 2,000 years ago! Now, God does not love your sin, He does not love the fact that you are running away from Him instead of running to Him, but He loves you! In other words, God hates the sin but loves the sinner. He still loves you. Yes, YOU!

"In this the love of God was made manifest (displayed) where we are concerned: in that God

sent His Son, the only begotten or unique [Son], into the world so that we might live through Him. In this is love: not that we loved God, but that He loved us and sent His Son to be the propitiation (the atoning sacrifice) for our sins." (1 John 4:9-10)

You see, it is not about what you have done or what you did but, it is about what Jesus did for you! That's what will cause God to never stop loving you. Jesus took your place on the cross at Calvary, He took upon Himself your sins and mine, all our sins both those of the past, present and future. He took all of them upon Him on the cross when He died for us.

We couldn't have earned it, we couldn't have carried our sins by ourselves, and we couldn't have saved ourselves. No man can! And we didn't deserve what He did for us either but yet, He so loved us that He chose willingly, to do it for us, to go all the way to set us free from the bondage of sin and set us free from the grip of the enemy the devil. Because of His great love for us.

"But God shows and clearly proves His [own] love for us by the fact that, while we were still sinners, Christ (the Messiah, the Anointed One) died for us. Therefore, since we are now justified (acquitted, made righteous and brought into right relationship with God) by Christ's blood, how much more [certain is it that] we shall be saved by Him from the indignation and wrath of God." (Romans 5:8-9)

You see, it was because of God's awesome love for us that He made the exchange for us. Putting His Son Jesus, to die for our sins when He was sinless and blameless... And so, instead of holding us under His judgment for our sins, He placed His Son under judgment in our place.

The Bible clearly says that, Jesus was despised and rejected and forsaken by men. He was acquainted with grief and sickness. He bore our griefs (sickness, weakness and distress) and carried our sorrows and pains [of punishment] He was wounded for our transgressions.

He was bruised for our guilt and iniquities; the chastisement [needful to obtain] peace and well-being for us was upon Him, and with His stripes [that wounded] Him we are healed and made whole. (Isaiah 53:3-5)

What an exchange! You see, Jesus was punished and condemned that, we may be forgiven and set free. He was made sin, though He was sinless, that we may be made the righteousness of God.

He bore our shame that we may be confident and have a good self-esteem. He was rejected that we may be accepted and approved by God our Father. He endured our poverty, became poor that we might enjoy His abundance and enjoy life to the full.

He was wounded that we might be healed and made whole. He took the curse of the law that, we might receive the blessing of God and live in freedom and liberty. He died for us that we might live and have eternal life with Him.

And all because He loved and still loves you and me. What an exchange! What a priceless exchange, and all because of His great love for you and me!

Friend, Jesus Christ came and exchanged His life for ours.

Everything that we could ever do that doesn't measure up to God's perfect will for us was taken away when He died for us. In other words, He paid the price for us, and through Him, we can now be loved by God. What an exchange! And yes, He did it out of pure love for us. For you and for me!

God loves you friend, but you have to receive His love. He would never force it on you. Receive it today, so that no matter your circumstances and challenges, no matter what you are going through, you can begin to experience His love that is so soothing, peaceful and enduring.

Never forget that, God loves you and me not because of who we are, what we have achieved and how we have performed etc. But because of what Jesus did for us! And the good news is, there is nothing you and I can do to stop God from loving us!

Never base His love for you on your feelings!

God's love for us should never be based on our feelings. You see, feelings come and feelings go. Feelings do change and especially when we are sad, upset and even tired.

Besides, we get moody at times based on how we feel, the weather, change in environment, illness and based on our circumstances but God's love for you never changes! His love for you remains constant regardless of whether you feel it or not.

And His love for us is certainly not blind and should not be based on our feelings! God loves us not because He doesn't see our faults, but He loves us because, He has made the decision to love us and does not look at our faults but only sees us through His Son Jesus and what He did for us.

In other words, it's not whether we are good or bad that causes God to love us, but He loves us regardless of our faults and weaknesses not because He can't see them, but He has made the decision to see us only through the blood of His Son Jesus Christ.

And yes, sometimes we do feel love by the outward show of it but God wants us to believe in His love for us not based on how we feel or our feeling it but He wants us to know it from our heart and not just from our heads!

He wants us to know that He loves us regardless of how we feel. We are not to depend on our feelings and emotions because they change but God remains the same for ever.

His Word remains the same for ever. And if He says in His Word that He loves us, we are to take His Word on it regardless of how we feel. And He wants us to experience His love for us, an experiential knowing of His love for us.

People change, things change, the weather changes, laws change, our feelings and emotions change but He wants us to know that, regardless of where we are at right now, regardless of our circumstances, we should believe in the truth that, His love for us will never change or fail and that, we can truly depend on Him to be there for us no matter what.

Friend, God has made a promise to love you and me, to be with us, to forgive us when we ask Him to, to hear our prayers. He has promised to never leave us nor forsake us and all He wants from us, is to believe in Him, to believe in His Word and in His love for us.

He wants us to have a relationship with Him. God wants to be faithful to us and show us His kindness and tender mercies.

"The Lord is my Rock, my Fortress and my deliverer; my God, my keen and firm strength in whom I will trust and take refuge, my shield and the horn of my salvation, my High Tower." (Psalms 18:2)

When you have an understanding of God's love for you, you will be able to stand strong and remain at peace and victorious regardless of your circumstances and challenges, knowing that God loves you and that He will help you because He loves you.

Do not believe the lie of the devil that God doesn't love you or that, God is too busy to help you or think about you. God cares about every little detail of your life!

"...For He [God] Himself has said, I will not in any way fail you nor give you up nor leave you without support. [I will] not, [I will] not, [I will] not, in any degree leave you helpless nor forsake not let [you] down (relax my hold on you)!" (Hebrews 13:5)

God has given us His gift of love. We didn't earn it or deserve it but He chose to freely give it to us. Some people have received His love and some have not or just refuse to receive it. I have received His love for me and it has changed my life for ever.

I am loved of God and I know it! I love God and I know He loves me! Please receive His love into your heart today. It is His desire that we fully understand and grasp how much He loves us. And know that He is concerned about us in every way. He is concerned about every single details of our lives.

"For as the heavens are high above the earth, so great are His mercy and loving kindness toward those who reverently and worshipfully fear Him." (Psalms 103: 11)

"For though the mountains should depart and the hills be shaken or removed, yet my love and kindness shall not depart from you, nor shall my covenant of peace and completeness be removed, says the Lord, who has compassion on you." (Isaiah 54:10)

Friend, God loves you and nothing will ever stop Him from loving you because of what Jesus did for us! He loves us so much that, He has engraved us upon the palms of His hand.

"Behold, I have indelibly imprinted (tattooed a picture of) you on the palm of each of my hands. [O Zion] your walls are continually before me." (Isaiah 49:16)

God loves you friend, you are so valuable in His sight. You matter to God, He will never ever stop loving you and above all, He wants to have fellowship with you. He wants you to have a personal relationship with Him so He can love you even more and show you His goodness!

Please say this out loud to yourself: GOD LOVES ME! GOD LOVES ME! GOD LOVES ME! – Amen.

Chapter four

GOD CAN STILL REACH YOU

Friend, I don't know how far gone you think you are away from God but, the good news is that, God can still reach you wherever you are, no matter how far gone you think you are away from Him.

God can still reach you and in fact, He has been reaching out to you all this while just waiting for you to call out to Him, to make the decision to ask Him into your life. You are never so far away that God cannot reach you.

You see, no matter the amount of atrocities you think you may have committed in the past or in the present, God can still reach you. He will never give up on you until the day you take your last breath. He will continue to love you and love you! It was for someone like you that Jesus came to die for. God will never stop loving you.

You are still so valuable and precious in His sight and He truly loves you in spite of you. In spite of all the negative or good things you have done. God still loves you and wants to reach out to you right where you are if you will allow Him.

"In this the love of God was manifested toward us, that God has sent His only begotten Son into the World, that we might live through Him. In this is love, not that we loved God, but that He loved us and sent His Son to be the propitiation for our sins." (1 John 4:9-10 NKJV)

Propitiation means, "To atone or make amends for." Jesus Christ came into the world and died in our place (atoned for our personal sins) so that, we could become free from the penalty of sin, which is eternal death. That is, eternal separation from God.

But, Jesus died so that you and I can be saved and have fellowship with God forever. You see, Satan's plan over your life is to continue to condemn you and keep you feeling bad and miserable about your life both present and past.

His plan is to get you to believe that, you have gone too far away for God to reach you. But the devil is a liar! He wants you to think and believe that God could never love someone like you or forgive you but, he is a liar.

No matter the sins you have committed or no matter how good you may think you are, it doesn't change anything and will never change God's mind from loving you. God will always love you no matter what! Because of what Jesus did for you.

We all at one point in time or the other, had / have lost our lives to the devil, we all at one point in time or the other, have / had lived in sin but that's the reason why Jesus came to die for us.

He paid the penalty for our sins with His life so that He would redeem us back to God, to have and enjoy eternal fellowship with God. Jesus literally bought us back to God! You and I now belong to God and not the devil.

God loves you so much and He will never stop loving you because of what Jesus did for you and me. Regardless of what you've done, God does not condemn you! He will never condemn you. Condemnation only comes from the devil and from our sinful nature.

"There is therefore now no condemnation to those who are in Christ Jesus, who do not walk according to the flesh, but according to the spirit." (Romans 8:1)

To walk according to the flesh is to walk according to your feelings, emotions and according to the world standards and dictates of the devil. But to walk according to the spirit is to walk according to the Word of God, according to His spirit and His instructions.

God through His Son Jesus, came to give us life, abundant life, life to the full with nothing missing and nothing broken. But the devil is a thief, who comes to steal, kill and to destroy if you allow him. But the truth is, if you are not in Christ Jesus, you cannot resist the devil.

"The thief does not come except to steal and to kill and to destroy. I have come that they may have life,

and that they may have it more abundantly." (John 10:10)

Can God really love somebody like me?

There was a certain man in the Bible called Saul, before he was later called Paul. He persecuted Christians, the church, opposing the faith of our Lord Jesus so much and with everything within his power.

He lived by the letter of the law rather than through an understanding of God's love, because, he didn't know God and His Son Jesus.

But despite all of the wicked terrible things he did to the churches and to many men and women and their children, he found God's grace and accepted God's love and forgiveness through His Son Jesus. He got born again after receiving Jesus Christ into his heart and life.

"As for Saul, he made havoc of the church, entering every house, and dragging off men and women, committing them to prison." (Acts 8:3 NKJV)

"Then Saul, still breathing threats and murder against the disciples of the Lord, went to the high priest and asked letters from him to the synagogues of Damascus, so that if he found any who were of the way, whether men or women, he might bring them bound to Jerusalem." (Acts 9:1-2 NKJV)

Friend, God never stopped loving him even when he hurt the church and destroyed Christian families and all. God still loved him even then but of cause, God didn't love what he was doing, but God still loved him and was reaching out to him until he (Paul) made the decision to receive God's love and forgiveness.

God loves you. And as tough as it may be to believe, it is the absolute truth. God loves you! Friend, God truly loves YOU! Saul, then was or could have been regarded or likened to a terrorist. But when he found God's love and accepted it, his whole life changed for ever and in his own words he said,

"This is a faithful saying and worthy of all acceptance, that Christ Jesus came into the world

to save sinners, of whom I am chief." (1 Timothy 1:15 NKJV)

"I have been crucified with Christ; it is no longer I who live, but Christ lives in me; and the life which I now live in the flesh I live by faith in the Son of God, who loved me and gave Himself for me," (Galatians 2:20 NKJV)

"Oh, but I have done really terrible things in my life...I don't think that God could still love someone like me." Friend, God loves you regardless of what you have done. He may not like what you have done, but He loves you anyway.

It was for someone like you that Jesus came into the world to die for! Yes, it was for you that He came to die for because He loves you and will never stop loving you. Let's look at another person in the Bible, let's look at David. David could have been called a murderer and he was then, and an adulterer and at a point a hypocrite when he tried to hide his sins.

But you see, later in David's life, the Bible records that, God called him a man after His Own heart

(God's heart) because, David came to repentance before God and received God's love, mercy and forgiveness.

Your past failures and experiences may make you feel unworthy of God's love, God's attention and His forgiveness, but that's not God's will for you. In other words, it's not God's will for you to condemn yourself because of your past mistakes, failures and experiences.

God wants you to forget them and just simply receive His unconditional love and forgiveness. God is love. His very nature is love and He will never stop loving you and all He requires of you is to receive His love. He is reaching out to you right now…He loves you!

"But God demonstrates His Own love toward us, in that while we were still sinners, Christ died for us." (Romans 5:8 NKJV)

You are worthy of God's love because of what Jesus did for you. God loves you and the Bible clearly says that God loves you. He has proven His love for us by sending His only Son, Jesus to die on the cross about 2,000 years ago and He has given us His abundant life through His Son Jesus.

God will never stop loving you because of what Jesus did for you. He is reaching out to you right now. Please receive His unconditional love for you! And maybe you were born again before, you had received God's love and forgiveness but later drifted back into the world and into sin.

God still loves you and wants to reach out to you. He has been reaching out to you all this while, patiently waiting for you to open up your heart to Him. You can rededicate your life back to God even today, right now.

You see, sometimes, life can hit us with unexpected situations that makes us to begin to think and wonder and ask ourselves if God still loves us. He still loves you friend, He still loves you and that's one of the reasons you are reading this little book to know that He still loves you and He is eagerly waiting for you to receive His love and forgiveness.

It's the devil working on your mind, condemning you and getting you to think and believe that God could never love you again. The devil doesn't want you to know and receive God's amazing love for you.

He comes with all the negative thoughts saying, "If God truly loves you, then why are you facing all of the challenges you are going through? Why did God get you into the mess you are in? Why didn't God do something about it or prevent it from happening and so on and so forth.

Friend, God is good, He is a good God and He still loves you period! And above all, He has never been responsible for all your mess and negative experiences. The devil was and your wrong choices and decisions were!

The Bible says that, God does not tempt us with evil. God is not the one responsible for all your hardships, pain and negative experiences. In fact, if not for God still watching over you, it would have been worst and you probably would have been long dead.

You see, the best we can do is ask God for His forgiveness and receive His love. God only wants the best for you. He has said in His Word,

"For I know the thoughts and plans that I have for you, says the Lord, thoughts and plans for welfare and peace and not for evil, to give you hope in your final outcome." (Jeremiah 29:11)

The Bible says that, God does not tempt us with evil. *"Let no one say when he is tempted, "I am tempted by God." For God cannot be tempted by evil, nor does He Himself tempt anyone. But each one is tempted when he is drawn away by his own desires and enticed." (James 1:13-14 NKJV)*

"Every good and every perfect gift is from above, and comes down from the father of lights, with whom there is no variation or shadow of turning." (James 1:17 NKJV)

Friend, every evil, every negative situation and experiences in your life is not from God. You know, when things go wrong in our lives, we easily point fingers at something else or someone else as the cause of it and a lot of times, we point fingers at God.

That, He is or was the cause of it or that, He brought it to teach you and I a lesson. That's a lie from the pit of hell! God will never use anything negative to teach us a lesson or help us. Never!

The Bible says that, rather, it's His goodness towards us that causes us to repent. So rather than deal negatively with us, when we do bad things or when we are in the wrong, God chooses rather to do us good, more good!

"Or are you [so blind as to] trifle with and presume upon and despise and underestimate the wealth of His kindness and forbearance and long-suffering patience?

Are you unmindful or actually ignorant [of the fact] that God's kindness is intended to lead you to repent (to change your mind and inner man to accept God's will)? (Romans 2:4)

When things happen, it's always wise to know and find out why such things happened. A lot of times and almost all the time, it is caused by our wrong decisions and choices, our ignorance and deceptions from the devil. God loves you and still loves you. His love for you will not change regardless of all you have done.

His love for you will never change and cannot fail. He is a loving God and He wants to be a Father to you, a Father who loves you so very much. He wants to be good to you, to care for you and have great relationship with you more than you could ever imagine.

He loves you and it was because of His love for you that He sent His Son Jesus to die for you and me on the cross. But bless God, Jesus died and rose again from the dead and that's why we can be loved, accepted and approved by God!

Do not allow the devil sell you his lies that, God could never love and save someone like you, and that, you are not worthy of God's love but of hell. Don't allow the devil to get you to believing the lie that, you are doomed for hell.

Remember, he is a liar and the father of all lies. God will never stop loving you because of what Jesus did for you!

Chapter five

WILL GOD SEND ME TO HELL?

No! Absolutely not. God will never send you or anyone to hell. God is love. His very nature is love. He does not have love, He is Love and He is a good God! His love for you and me is an everlasting love, a love that will never fail or change, a pure love that is full of compassion for us.

God didn't create hell for human beings. He created hell for the devil and his fallen angels. Jesus did talk about hell in several scriptures in the Bible. He did say that, it is a place of eternal torment. And He does know more about hell than you and I could ever know.

"The Son of man will send forth His angels, and they will gather out of his kingdom all causes of offence [persons by whom others are drawn into error or sin] and all who do iniquity and act wickedly, and will cast them into the furnace of

fire; there will be weeping and wailing and grinding of teeth... so it will be at the close and consumption of the age.

The angels will go forth and separate the wicked from the righteous (those who are upright and in right standing with God) and cast them [the wicked] into the furnace of fire; there will be weeping and wailing and grinding of teeth." (Matthew 13:41-43; 49-50)

See also, (Mark 9:43-47), Being religious cannot save you and I from hell, going to church every now and again cannot save us from hell, wearing a cross and putting your Bible under your pillow cannot either.

Neither will saying the psalms or holding a rosary and saying the Hail Mary confession. Nothing and nobody can save us from hell except Jesus Christ. Only He can save you and me from hell and He has already made a way out for us!

Friend, regardless of what you do, God will never stop loving you and He will never send anyone to hell. Far beyond the issue of hell, more than anything, God wants relationship, fellowship with you! Now, let me tell you why God will not send you or anyone to hell.

<u>You make the choice to go to hell, not God!</u>

"I call heaven and earth to witness this day against you that I have set before you life and death, the blessings and the curses; therefore, choose life that you and your descendants may live." (Deuteronomy 30:19)

In other words, God has put the choice in your hands to either live for Him and enjoy eternal life with Him through His Son Jesus in Heaven or refuse to live for Him by rejecting His Son Jesus, and all that He did for you and me and then send yourself into hell when you physically die, by your own wrong choices and deceptions of the devil you chose to believe and accept.

Jesus paid the ultimate price and sacrifice for you and me when He died on the cross for us, and rose again from the dead to set us free from the law and from the bondage of sin.

Refusing to believe what He did for you and receiving His love and forgiveness, you (not God) are sending yourself to hell when you die. God will never send you to hell because, He has put that decision in your own hands!

Friend, God who is loving and full of compassion towards us, has put the choice right in our own hands to make the decision ourselves on where we would spend eternity. However, He has also, as a good and loving Father that He is, helped us to know the right choice to make.

Whether or not we follow His advice and help already provided is left to us. We cannot blame anyone or blame God but ourselves if we choose to make the wrong choice, even when God has really made it so clear what choice we should make to save us from hell.

"Whose minds the god of this age has blinded, who do not believe, lest the light of the gospel of the glory of God, should shine on them." (2 Corinthians 4:4)

You see, God has done and He is still doing everything possible to keep us out of hell. He originally created hell for the devil and his fallen angels and not for people, you and me. But, the devil is working so hard to deceive God's people to believe a lie.

The devil is deceiving people about the truth of what God did for us through His Son Jesus, deceiving men and women, boys and girls not to accept what Jesus did for them on Calvary, not to accept Him into their lives as Lord and Saviour, which will eventually get them into hell. The devil is a deceiver!

"So the great dragon was cast out, that serpent of old, called the devil and Satan, who deceives the whole world; he was cast to the earth, and his angels were cast out with him." (Revelation 12:9, NKJV)

"Now the serpent was more subtle and crafty than any living creature of the field which the Lord God had made..." (Genesis 3:1)

The Bible clearly says that, God's will for us is not for anyone of us to perish but, that we might all come to the knowledge of His Son Jesus and receive His love, His forgiveness and all He did for us.

"The Lord does not delay and is not tardy or slow about what He promises, according to some people's conception of slowness, but He is long suffering (extraordinarily patient) toward you, not desiring that any should perish, but that all should turn to repentance." (2 Peter 3:9)

"For I know the thoughts and plans that I have for you, says the Lord, thoughts and plans for welfare and peace and not evil, to give you hope in your final outcome." (Jeremiah 29:11)

God created hell long before we were created and it was all because of His great love for us that He, being moved with compassion for us, sent His only Son, Jesus to come to the earth to die on the cross for us, and to pay the ransom for our sins.

So that we do not have to suffer and be destroyed by the devil and end up in hell. We could never ever have been able to pay the ransom by ourselves and we were not worthy to pay it either because we were full of sin.

Jesus suffered and went to the cross so He could set us free from the bondage of sin, and from eternity in hell. He has provided forgiveness for us and has made us whole again but we must simply believe in Him and what He did for us and receive Him into our lives. Yes, it's that simple.

God has done everything possible to make a way of escape for us from hell. And yes, He has given us the power to make our choice on this, to accept Jesus and all He did for us and be saved or reject His love and forgiveness and send ourselves to hell, by rejecting Jesus. He will never force us against our will.

Friend, you don't have to go to hell. It's not worth it. It's not your sins that will take you to hell, it's not what you have done or have not done. It certainly isn't all the crimes and bad stuff you have done.

Friend, it's not about how innocent you are or how good you are or how well you have lived your life.

Neither is it based on your charitable deeds. It's not our self-righteousness either. It is refusing to receive Jesus Christ into your heart as your Lord and Saviour.

It's your choice and decision of refusing to receive His love and forgiveness that will send you to hell. But you don't have to go that way. Jesus has already made a way of escape for you. It is believing in the finished work of Jesus on the cross.

It is receiving Jesus into our lives! Accepting Jesus as our Lord and Saviour! All you need to do is believe in Him, that He is the Son of God and that He died for your sins and rose again from the dead for you, and confess it with your mouth as you believe in your heart.

Make Him Lord and saviour of your life and you shall be saved…even from hell. Jesus is the door and the only way to God and to heaven. Someone once said that, "people do not have to do something to go to hell.

They just have to do nothing to go to hell." They probably are right. You see, if you do nothing about receiving Jesus into your life, you will surely be doing nothing to go to hell. It's not worth it!

Hell is real and so is Heaven, but God's love for you and all that Jesus came to the earth to do for you is even more real and more important in your life right now. Beyond the thought of hell and all that, the most important thing God desires for you is that, you have a relationship with Him!

God loves you and He wants the best for you. Do you want the best for yourself? If yes, then it's that easy. The first step to have God's best in your life is to receive His best, His Son Jesus.

"For the wages of sin is death, but the [bountiful] free gift of God is eternal life through (in union with) Jesus Christ our Lord." (Romans 6:23)

Do not allow anything or anyone to stop you from having a relationship with God through His Son Jesus Christ, through their false philosophies and fables. Don't allow the devil to stop you with his lies.

It's just not worth it! Hell is real but knowing Jesus Christ based on His love for you is more important. He loves you and wants the very best for you. His love and forgiveness awaits your response.

"And if anyone's [name] was not found recorded in the Book of Life, he was hurled into the lake of fire." (Revelations 20:15)

God loves you so very much. You matter to Him, His LOVE, will never stop loving you regardless and He can still reach you no matter how far away you may think you have gone away from Him. He is reaching out to you today, right now. He has been reaching out to you all along.

His will for you is to spend eternity with Him in Heaven and enjoy life to the full even while here on earth. He will never send you to hell but you are the one who can determine where you spend eternity by the choices you make.

He has given you the free will to make the choice yourself but He wants you to make the right choice. The right choice is to reach out to Him today, make the right choice friend, and get into a personal relationship with God. He wants to love you even more and show you His great salvation.

Chapter six

GOD WANTS RELATIONSHIP WITH YOU

To come into a personal relationship with God through His Son Jesus, is His great desire for you. In other words, God has made it possible for you to come into a relationship with Him through His son Jesus because of His great love for you.

He loves you and longs to save you. He has made your forgiveness possible through the death and resurrection of His Son Jesus, which cost Jesus enormously. It was no easy journey for Him, but He went all the way for you regardless of all the pain, shame and all He knew He would go through because of His love for you.

Friend, God created you for a purpose and it was primarily to fellowship with Him, to enjoy His sweet presence. He created you to have a great

Father – Child relationship with Him. You cannot fellowship with Him, earn His acceptance and love by yourself effort.

That's why Jesus came to do it for you and me, what we could never do for ourselves and by ourselves. He came to connect and reconcile us back to God our Heavenly Father, which was and is only through Him and no other.

"He saved us, not because of any works of righteousness that we had done, but because of His own pity and mercy, by [the] cleansing [bath] of the new birth (regeneration) and renewing of the Holy Spirit..." (Titus 3:5)

"He personally bore our sins in His [own] body on the tree [as on an altar and offered Himself on it], that we might die (cease to exist) to sin and live to righteousness. By His wounds you have been healed." (1 Peter 2:24)

God's desire for you is to have fellowship with Him, a personal relationship with Him. To know Him and to love Him back because He loves you. To fellowship with Him involves communicating with Him throughout your day.

Just like you do with a close friend, best friend or close family member whom you love. He wants you to spend time with Him and you can do that by spending time with His Word, the Bible. He is His Word and His Word is Him. He wants you to be grateful for all that He did for you and all that He is doing in your life even when you can't seem to see it. He is working on your case.

Friend, when you get to know God for yourself, when you get to know His love for you and receive His love, it changes you and changes the way you want to live your life. It will change your life and circumstances for good. He has given us His life and He wants us to give Him ours.

He wants to love you and care for your every need and give you the best life you could ever dream of or imagine. He is concerned about every single detail of your life. He wants to help you, answer your prayer, provide for you, and heal your body and so much more.

However, these and more can only be possible, when you know Him and have fellowship with Him, when you have a personal relationship with Him through His Son Jesus. How? By believing in Him by faith, believing in what His Son Jesus did for you and receive Him by faith into your life as your Lord and personal Saviour.

"For we do not have a High Priest who is unable to understand and sympathise and have a shared feeling with our weaknesses and infirmities and liability to the assaults of temptation. But one who has been tempted in every respect as we, yet without sinning.

Let us then fearlessly and confidently and boldly draw near to the throne of grace (the throne of God's unmerited favour to us sinners), that we may receive mercy [for our failures] and find grace to help in good time for every need [appropriate help and well- timed help, coming just when we need it]." (Hebrews 4:15-16)

Jesus loves you and understands what you are going through because He had gone through it and much more than you could ever imagine and that's why He is the perfect example for us to follow.

Regardless of what you have done, God will never hold it against you because, He has already provided forgiveness for you for your past, present and future sins. But, you must believe and receive it. (Please see Colossians 2:13-14)

God loves you and doesn't condemn you! The Bible says in Romans 8:1 that, *"there is therefore now, no condemnation (no adjudging guilty of wrong) for those who are in Christ Jesus…" (Romans 8:1)*

"For God did not send the Son into the world in order to judge (to reject, to condemn, to pass sentence on) the world, but that the world might find salvation and be made safe and sound through Him." (John 3:17)

Making the decision to make Jesus your Lord and Saviour is the most important decision you will ever make in this life. Through His grace, He has already provided salvation and everything you will ever need to enjoy the best in life.

Get into relationship with God today

Friend, you do not know what your tomorrow will bring or be like. If you were to die today, tonight, are you sure you will make it to heaven and be with the Lord or to hell where there is torment? The only way you can be sure of your tomorrow and be sure where you would be when you die is to accept the Lord Jesus into your heart, and into your life today.

It is never too late for you right now that you still have breathe. You have nothing to lose but all to gain. We all believe in something but the question is, do we believe in the right thing. Friend, believe in the Lord Jesus today.

When you have a personal relationship with God through His Son Jesus, by asking Him to come into your heart, your life will get exciting because, not only will you be loved of God and by the Father, but, God also puts in you His love through His Spirit to love people.

When you get born again, by receiving Jesus into your life, you get into the family of God. And with

God on your side, you have what it takes to become successful and to defeat the devil every time and the devil knows it.

That's why he is doing his very best to stop you from hearing about Jesus and God's love for you. That's why he is doing everything possible to stop you from receiving God's love, and His Son Jesus Christ into your heart and trying to get you to doubt the love of God for you by manipulating your feelings and lying to you.

Remember, the devil is a thief and a deceiver! That's who he is and he is the father of lies!

"The thief comes only in order to steal and kill and destroy. I came that they may have life and enjoy life, and have it in abundance (to the full, till it overflows)." (John 10:10)

Today, if you have not yet received Jesus into your life, why not do that right now. If you have never asked Him personally to come into your heart and be your Lord and saviour, this is your opportunity, your chance to do it.

It's easy. All you have to do is believe in your heart what the Bible says, what God's Word promises concerning Jesus. Let me tell you what God promises to you and me. God's Word promises that,

"That, if you confess with your mouth the Lord Jesus and believe in your heart that God has raised Him from the dead, you will be saved. For with the heart one believes unto righteousness, and with the mouth confession is made unto salvation...For whoever calls on the name of the Lord shall be saved." (Romans 10:9-10; 13 NKJV)

Prayer for salvation

Please pray this prayer out loud with me.

Dear God, I come to you now in the name of Jesus to receive salvation and eternal life. I believe in my heart and confess out loud with my mouth that Jesus is your Son.

I believe that, He died on the cross for my sins and that You raised Him up from the dead. I receive Jesus now into my heart and make Him my Lord and Saviour.

Jesus, I confess that, you are my Lord and Saviour. I believe in my heart that, God raised you up from the dead. By faith I ask you to come into my heart and I receive you into my heart now.

I welcome you into my life as my Lord and saviour. Thank you for saving me. I confess with my mouth now that I am saved and born again. I am now a child of God! Thank you Lord.

Welcome to the family!

Congratulations friend! You are now born again and now a part of God's wonderful family. Remember, it does not matter whether you felt anything or not when you prayed this prayer.

If you believed in your heart that you received Jesus into your life, you did. Start now to develop your relationship with God by taking time to pray to Him. Prayer is communication with God, talking to him and listening for Him to talk back to you.

The Word of God says that, Faith comes by hearing and hearing by the Word of God. Romans 10:17. Everything you need to know about God is in His Word.

Look into His Word daily and find God's plan and purpose for your life. The answers to every question you may have and every solution you need to the challenges of your life is found in God's Word!

Please contact us if you prayed this prayer. We would love to rejoice with you and send you a free gift that will help you to understand and grow in your new birth and in your relationship with God.

Find a Bible to start reading so you can know more about God and all that God says about you. If you do not have one and cannot afford one, please contact us via our Ministry at – **Infallible Word Ministries** and we will send you a free Bible.

Feel free to pass this book on to someone else who has a desire to know the Lord Jesus and His unconditional love for them. God bless you!

For more details about Infallible Word Ministries and how to contact us, please visit our website. We would love to connect with you, stand with you in prayer and encourage you in your faith and walk with God.

INFALLIBLE WORD MINISTRIES

www.infallibleword.org.uk

About the author

Rosemary Francis Okolo practiced as a Barrister and Solicitor in the federal Republic of Nigeria, for several years before relocating to the United Kingdom. She is a Music Minister, a song writer, Worship Leader, an Author, Entrepreneur and a woman with a passion for God.

In addition, her desire and goal is to write great quality, thought provoking books based on God's Word that would connect people to the truth of His Word. Bringing healing, encouragement and empower them in whatever circumstances or challenges that they may be going through.

Rosemary is a simple woman who has a passion to reach out to her generation, the Youth and women, especially hurting women. She and her husband Charles Okolo are founders of Infallible Word Ministries. Its mission is to share the infallible Word of God and His unconditional love to all with integrity.

To teach young believers worldwide who they are in

Christ Jesus and how to live a victorious life in their covenant rights and privileges, and reach out to hurting people with provision for spirit, soul and body.

They are happily married and both live together in the United Kingdom, with their three blessed Children. Please visit Rosemary's website for more details.

<u>www.rosemaryokolo.org</u>

Printed in Great Britain
by Amazon